CW01512645

Original title:
Velvet Needles Around the Witch Sail

Copyright © 2025 Swan Charm
All rights reserved.

Author: Johan Kirsipuu
ISBN HARDBACK: 978-1-80562-432-5
ISBN PAPERBACK: 978-1-80563-953-4

Enchanted Tales in Thread and Fabric

In twilight's hush, the loom did sing,
Of woven dreams, and tales to bring.
Each thread a whisper, soft and bright,
Creating worlds beyond the night.

A tapestry of magic spun,
By nimble fingers, one by one.
In every knot, a secret's grace,
A time-worn smile, a gentle face.

From silken strands of stars above,
To cotton clouds, a tale of love.
Adventures dance in colors bold,
As destinies in fabric unfold.

With each new stitch, a heartbeat flows,
In patterns rich, the story grows.
A hero's journey, lost, then found,
In woven threads, their fate is bound.

By candlelight, the shadows play,
In every corner, dreams at bay.
With needle sharp and heart so true,
The stories weave, old and new.

The Weaving of Night's Mysteries

Beneath the veil of midnight's grace,
The stars emerge, their twinkling face.
In shadows deep, creation sways,
As night unveils her secret ways.

A tapestry of dreams takes flight,
In whispers soft, enchanting night.
Each silver thread a wish concealed,
In moonlit fabric, fate revealed.

With every stitch a story spun,
Of love and loss, of battles won.
A darkened loom where shadows creep,
In woven tales, the heart must weep.

As dawn approaches, threads unwind,
Yet mysteries of night entwined.
For in the depth of fabric's fold,
The night keeps secrets yet untold.

So come, dear friend, and take a thread,
Join hands with dreams, let fears be shed.
For in each weave of night's embrace,
A world awaits, a secret place.

Nightfall's Lament in Stitch and Thread

In shadows deep, the needle weaves,
A tale of woe that night conceives.
With whispered threads, the past takes flight,
As memories dance in the pale moonlight.

Each stitch a sigh, in silence sown,
A tapestry of dreams overthrown.
Yet hope remains in every seam,
A fragile stitch of a forgotten dream.

The fabric bears the weight of tears,
A cloak of sorrow, woven fears.
But through the night, a spark ignites,
A glimpse of dawn, through darkest nights.

As shadows fade, the colors blend,
A story told, with each intent.
The night may fade, but not its thread,
In every heart, the myriad spread.

Crafting Charms in the Heart of Night

In the stillness, whispers stir,
Crafting charms that softly purr.
Moonlit spells in shadows grim,
With every pulse, the shadows swim.

A dash of light, a sprinkle of dark,
Weaving magic, the night's own spark.
With deft embrace, the clock ticks slow,
In secret havens where echoes flow.

Chasing starlight, dreams unfurl,
As midnight bells ring, thoughts swirl.
The heart beats loud in this sacred rite,
Crafting charms in the heart of night.

In bottles glimmering, potions gleam,
Brewed in silence from woven dream.
A mixture rare of love and fright,
Adventure blooms then takes its flight.

The Ties that Bind in Dusky Fabric

Stitched in twilight, threads entwine,
In dusky fabric, secrets shine.
The ties that bind in shadows cast,
A saga told, from first to last.

Each fiber hums a silent song,
Of places lost, where we belong.
In every fold, a story weaves,
A bond that lives in what one believes.

As night unfolds its velvet shroud,
The heartbeats murmur, soft yet loud.
With gentle care, the hands employ,
To stitch the seams of love and joy.

Yet darker threads remind and warn,
Of journeys ne'er before been worn.
In this fabric, truths unwind,
A map of dreams and ties that bind.

A Tapestry of Sinister Beauty

In shadows deep, a beauty grows,
A tapestry where darkness flows.
Each thread a smile, yet hides a frown,
In colors bright, the shadows drown.

With every weave, a story spins,
Of moonlit nights and whispered sins.
Beneath the charm, a hint of dread,
In this fabric, the tale is spread.

The patterns shift as daylight wavers,
A dance of lies, in time, it savors.
The sinister beauty pulls you close,
And in its grip, you feel morose.

Yet in the dark, allure does gleam,
A sinister smile, a haunting dream.
In twisted threads, love finds its call,
A tapestry that binds us all.

Patterns of the Enchanted Hearth

In the glow of ember light,
Patterns dance, soft and bright.
Whispers of tales long gone,
Embrace the night, life's sweet dawn.

Children gather, eyes aglow,
To the hearth, stories flow.
Shadows flicker, tales unfold,
Mysteries waiting to be told.

Through the warmth, enchantments weave,
A tapestry, we believe.
Each thread holds a secret bright,
Binding hearts in cozy night.

From the fire's tender kiss,
Dreams are forged, none to miss.
In the heart, the magic stirs,
As every ember softly purrs.

So let the hearth be our guide,
Where the ancient rites abide.
In the patterns, we will find,
The music of the heart and mind.

The Craft of the Shadows' Embrace

In the stillness of the night,
Shadows gather, taking flight.
With a flicker, spells arise,
Crafting dreams beneath the skies.

In the corners, secrets dwell,
Wrapped in the shadow's spell.
Glimmers of magic, hushed delight,
Whispers woven, soft as light.

Through the glen, the shadows creep,
Cradling wishes, thoughts so deep.
With each breath, the night unveils,
A world where whimsy never fails.

The craft unfolds in silent swirls,
Entwined in the dance of twirls.
With each heartbeat, shadows play,
In their arms, fears drift away.

So let the shadows form and blend,
In shadows' embrace, we transcend.
For in every fold and trace,
Lies the magic of the space.

Weaving Whispers of the Witching Hour

When the moon hangs low and bright,
Whispers weave through the night.
Magic churns in the cool air,
Serenade of secrets rare.

With a flick, the shadows spin,
Tales of wonder, where to begin?
In the depths of twilight's charms,
We find solace in nature's arms.

Wisps of light in the dark,
Ignite the dreams that leave their mark.
In the hush, enchantments bloom,
Banishing the shadows' gloom.

The witching hour holds the key,
To the magic that makes us free.
Embrace the whispers, soft and clear,
In every moment, the magic near.

So raise your hands to the night,
Let the whispers take their flight.
In the woven tales of lore,
Awaken the magic evermore.

The Ethereal Spinner of Ancient Tales

In the realm where legends twine,
The ethereal spinner does align.
Crafting fables, old and wise,
Beneath the stars, the spirits rise.

With a touch as light as air,
Threads of time drift without care.
Each story spun, a dream anew,
Awakening memories, tried and true.

The spinner's wheel turns ever slow,
Weaving echoes from long ago.
In the fabric, wonders blend,
A legacy that will not end.

Voices murmur in the night,
As the tales take glorious flight.
Every thread, a heart begets,
Binding past with no regrets.

So let the spinner craft her lore,
Of ancient worlds we can explore.
For in her tales, we understand,
The timeless magic of this land.

A Tapestry of Bewitching Whispers

In twilight's glow, the secrets sigh,
Where shadows dance and spirits fly.
An ancient tale begins to weave,
In every heart, a spark to believe.

Through moonlit paths and starlit dreams,
The world unfolds in silver seams.
Whispers drape like a velvet shawl,
Entwining souls, enchanting all.

A tapestry of hopes and fears,
Woven softly through the years.
With every thread, the stories blend,
A circle made that will not end.

In hidden corners, magic stirs,
The scent of wonder softly purrs.
A thread of fate, a twist of heart,
Each stitch a world, each tale a part.

So lift your gaze to skies afar,
Let dreams be guided by a star.
For in the weave of night's embrace,
Lies every wish, and every grace.

Shadows on the Wind's Canvas

Upon the breeze, the shadows play,
A canvas painted in shades of gray.
The whispers linger, soft as mist,
In every corner, secrets kissed.

With every gust, a story told,
Of dreams forgotten, brave and bold.
The sky, a brush of fading light,
Awakens tales that take to flight.

The dance of leaves in twilight's glow,
Holds magic secrets few may know.
Each flutter carries hope and fear,
A melody that calls us near.

In quiet moments, shadows sway,
Painting lives that drift away.
Each stroke a memory, fleeting fast,
A glimpse of futures, echoes past.

So walk the path where whispers blend,
Where shadows stretch and softly bend.
For in the wind, a heart may find,
The canvas vast, the ties that bind.

The Loom of Secrets and Serenity

In the loom of dawn, serenity weaves,
A tapestry of hopes, as daylight leaves.
With every whisper, peace unfolds,
In threads of silver, twilight holds.

Secrets linger in the morning air,
Dancing softly, light as a prayer.
Each strand a dream, each knot a wish,
A quiet heart finds joy in this.

The loom spins tales of fate and chance,
As petals fall in a gentle dance.
The world in stillness, softly sings,
Of hidden truths and quiet things.

With every weave, a story blooms,
A fragrant peace that softly looms.
And as the sun begins to rise,
A golden thread across the skies.

So let your heart be open wide,
Embrace the whispers, let them guide.
For in the loom of life we find,
A tapestry of soul entwined.

Twisted Yarns and Hidden Charms

In twilight's fold, the yarns entwine,
Twisted tales of fate divine.
Hidden charms in every fold,
A magic secret to behold.

With nimble fingers, fate does spin,
Stories wrought from deep within.
A tapestry of joy, of sorrow,
Each drawn tight binds the tomorrow.

Old spells linger in the loom,
Whispers carried through the gloom.
Each twist a note, each fiber sings,
Of ancient lore and other things.

Beneath the stars, a craft takes shape,
In woven dreams, the heart escapes.
The gentle rhythm, soft and warm,
Unveils the world, its hidden charm.

So draw the thread, embrace the art,
Let twisted yarns mend every heart.
For in the weave of dark and light,
Lies the magic of the night.

Riddles in a Witch's Quilt

In threads of midnight, secrets spin,
A quilt of whispers, where dreams begin.
Beneath the stars, the patterns weave,
A tale of magic, hard to believe.

With every stitch, a mystery grows,
Of fireflies dancing, and hidden prose.
The moonlight dances upon the seam,
Illuminating the heart of a dream.

Tales of potions and flickering wands,
Of enchanted gardens and far-off lands.
Each square a riddle, a challenge to face,
In this witch's quilt, you'll find your place.

Patterns of laughter, shadows of fears,
In the fabric of night, the magic appears.
Every unraveling, a truth to learn,
From the witch's quilt, the lanterns burn.

So gather close, let your heart be light,
Within this quilt, the world feels right.
For every riddle brings a sweet delight,
In the warmth of magic, our spirits take flight.

The Fabric of Bewitched Dreams

In the loom of night, where wishes stray,
A fabric crafted from dreams' soft play.
Each thread a story, each color a sigh,
Awakening worlds where lost visions lie.

This tapestry holds what the heart can't say,
Casting shadows on the light of day.
A shimmer of hope in the midnight air,
In silken whispers, our secrets laid bare.

Patterns of laughter, a stitch of fear,
Soft breath of magic, inviting us near.
With each pull of thread, a spell we weave,
In the fabric of dreams, we dare to believe.

Time drifts gently, a curious stream,
Not all is as simple as it may seem.
In enchanted threads, our fates intertwine,
The fabric of dreams, forever divine.

So close your eyes, let the visions fly,
In this bewitching world, we learn to try.
For every seam holds untold schemes,
Inside the fabric, the heart often gleams.

A Stitch in Shadows

In the twilight hues, shadows depart,
A stitch in darkness, a tale to impart.
With needles of silver, the night takes flight,
Crafting the phantoms that dance with the light.

Each whispering seam, a journey begun,
Through hidden realms that shun the sun.
In twilight's embrace, enchantments abide,
Where secrets and sorrows together collide.

Threads of remembrance, woven with care,
Echoes of laughter hang thick in the air.
In needles that sparkle with visions unseen,
A stitch in shadows, a world in between.

The fabric trembles with stories untold,
Of distant echoes and fortunes bold.
Each stitch a promise, each knot a regret,
In the shadowy folds, we gather, we bet.

So linger a moment, embrace what you find,
In the stitch of shadows, a tale intertwined.
For from the darkness, new light may rise,
In the depths of the stitching, a truth lies.

Threads of Enchantment and Mystery

In the heart of dusk where whispers play,
Threads of enchantment in colors sway.
Each twist a secret, each turn a spell,
Woven with care, a magical shell.

Mysteries flutter on a shimmering breeze,
As fairies giggle and wink from the trees.
With every fiber, a vision takes form,
In the fabric of night, we weather the storm.

Patterns emerge, like stories in flight,
Painting the canvas of dream-laden night.
Each thread a journey, each color a song,
In this woven realm, we all belong.

As shadows retreat, the stars wink in glee,
Revealing the wonders that we cannot see.
In the tapestry woven with laughter and tears,
Threads of enchantment unravel our fears.

So drape this cloak on your soul, let it glow,
For with every stitch, we learn, we grow.
In the realm of magic, and dreams set free,
Threads of enchantment weave destiny.

Threads of Enigma in the Night

In the twilight's grasp, they bloom,
Whispers weave along the loom,
Each thread a tale, each knot a sign,
Mysteries blend, entwined in time.

Stars blink softly, secrets shared,
Patterns dance, with magic bared,
A tapestry of dreams unfurls,
In the night, where silence swirls.

The owls hoot in solemn rhyme,
Crooning songs of bygone time,
Navigating paths adorned in light,
Weaving truth with threads of night.

From shadows deep, the stories rise,
Anchored strong in whispering ties,
Each twine a promise, a longing peak,
Revealing worlds that secrets seek.

Together they sew a fabric bright,
Guided by the moon's soft light,
In the night's embrace, they find their place,
Threads of enigma, an interlaced grace.

Incantations of a Stitched Heart

Behind the seams, the magic lies,
Stitches hold what seldom cries,
A heart once torn, now stitched anew,
Whispers echo, love breaks through.

With needle threaded by fate's own hand,
Each loop a spell across the land,
Binding fragments, mending old,
Stories woven, threads of gold.

In shadows cast by flickering flame,
The stitched heart beats, calls your name,
Incantations rise with every pull,
In crafted quiet, the world feels full.

Embroidered dreams in midnight's shade,
Symbolic words, spells are laid,
A tapestry where lovers meet,
Every stitch a bond, complete.

As daylight breaks through fabric thick,
The heart sings soft, a gentle trick,
In every seam, the stories flow,
Incantations of love, forever glow.

The Fisherman's Spell Under the Veil

Beneath the veil, the waters sigh,
A fisherman casts his net on high,
With every splash, a dream takes flight,
In rippling depths, shadows ignite.

He murmurs spells, the current swirls,
Where magic sways and mystery twirls,
Each fish a wish, glimmering bright,
Catching hope in the fading light.

The net holds stories of age-old fears,
Where laughter mingles with silent tears,
In careful hands, the sea's embrace,
Fisherman's craft, a timeless grace.

Under twilight's soft, enchanting veil,
Legend whispers the fisherman's tale,
As catch and current blend and weave,
In salty dreams, we dare believe.

The waves caress the shore with ease,
Where wishes linger on every breeze,
With a final cast, the night draws near,
The fisherman's spell, a song we hear.

Shadows That Stitch and Snare

In a world where shadows play,
Threads of dusk twine night and day,
They stretch and weave in crafty form,
Stitching silence, gathering storm.

With every snare, a secret caught,
In clever knots the darkness sought,
An echo of footsteps, soft and light,
In shadow's grasp, they take to flight.

Whispers linger in the gloom,
Each stitch a riddle, a hidden room,
Forming shapes our minds desire,
In their dance, the hearts transpire.

Crafted edges blur and blend,
Shadows craft the paths we send,
Stitching stories that softly glare,
Underneath the midnight air.

A fragile balance, a delicate thread,
Where shadows work and dreams are fed,
In the moon's embrace, they anchor where,
Life is stitched with a gentle care.

Gloomy Stitches Under the Stars

Under the quilt of deepest night,
Stitches weave dreams out of sight.
Moonlight flickers, shadows play,
In the silence, secrets lay.

Threads of silver, soft and thin,
Hold the whispers deep within.
Patterns of fate, tangled and tight,
Bring the eerie world to light.

With every knot, a tale is spun,
Of battles lost and victories won.
In the stillness, echoes call,
Of magic woven, never small.

Twilight lingers, breathes its sigh,
As stars blink softly in the sky.
Each stitch a promise, bright yet grim,
A tapestry that shadows brim.

Gather, gather, the tales of old,
Under the stars, a future unfolds.
In twilight's grasp, where hopes reside,
Gloomy stitches, our fates collide.

Shadows of the Needles' Dance

In the dark, the needles gleam,
Dancing shadows weave a dream.
Threads entwined like hearts that yearn,
In flickering firelight, secrets burn.

Silent whispers fill the room,
As shadows leap to cast the gloom.
Each stitch a language, rich and wide,
Of hidden truths we dare not hide.

Around the table, tales are spun,
By firelight's warmth, the work begun.
Eager fingers grasp the thread,
Of visions waking from the dead.

With every knot, a dancer sways,
In the stillness of endless days.
Softly weaving through time and space,
Shadows take form, and dreams embrace.

In twilight's glow, we craft our fate,
Needles weaving love, despair, innate.
In every stitch, the past resounds,
Shadows of needles in silent bounds.

The Craft of Whispers in Twilight's Veil

Twilight falls with a gentle grace,
Whispers linger in this place.
Threads of gold, like secrets spun,
Knit the fabric of everyone.

In the dusk where shadows creep,
Soft enchantments begin to seep.
Knit and purl, the rhythms flow,
In twilight's realm, we come to know.

Softly murmured, tales unfold,
Secrets whispered, dreams retold.
In every stitch, a heart laid bare,
A craft of whispers, pure and rare.

With every fiber, hopes unite,
Weaving futures in the night.
Twilight's veil, so rich and vast,
Holds the magic of the past.

So gather 'round and spin your tales,
In twilight's arms, where wonder prevails.
The craft of whispers draws us near,
In every stitch, the heart's sincere.

Gathering the Threads of Fate

In the stillness where shadows blend,
Threads of fate twist and bend.
Gathering colors, bright and bold,
Stories waiting to be told.

Through the needle, futures pass,
Woven gently, as the hours glass.
Every knot, a choice we make,
In time's embrace, the fabric takes.

From the quiet, echoes ring,
In each stitch, the world will sing.
We gather whispers of the hour,
Knit together, threads of power.

In the loom of life, we find our way,
With every motion, come what may.
Gathering tales beneath the skies,
In every pattern, the truth lies.

So stitch the threads with hope and care,
In the fabric of dreams, let us share.
Gathering fate, as stars ignite,
We weave the vision of our night.

Spells Sewn in Gloomy Hues

In shadowed corners where whispers creep,
The magic stirs, in silence deep.
With threads of night and twilight's sigh,
We weave our dreams, as stars drift by.

Through fabric dark, enchantments flow,
In hidden realms, where few dare go.
The weavers hum a haunting tune,
As shadows dance beneath the moon.

With needles sharp and hearts sincere,
We stitch the spells that dare to veer.
A tapestry of hopes unfurled,
In gloomy hues, we shape our world.

Each stitch a tale, each knot a fate,
Entwined with magic, we contemplate.
Through gloomy shades and whispered light,
We craft our stories, bold and bright.

So gather close, and lend your hand,
Together in this silent band.
For spells are sewn in every hue,
A quilt of dreams, just waiting for you.

Enigmatic Threads of the Night

In twilight's veil, the secrets hide,
With threads of silver, side by side.
Enigmas whispered in the breeze,
As night unfolds with gentle ease.

The stars above begin to gleam,
Awakening a distant dream.
A tapestry of twinkling lights,
That guides us through the shadowed nights.

Each cosmic stitch, a story spun,
Of battles lost and battles won.
In darkness, hope begins to rise,
On threads of night, we weave our ties.

The fabric rich with tales untold,
Of brave adventures, hearts so bold.
In every seam, a magic hums,
And beckons forth where wonder comes.

So let us roam where dreams collide,
In every thread, our fates abide.
The enigmatic night awaits
With whispers of enchanted states.

The Fabric of Forgotten Legends

In ancient looms, the whispers dwell,
Of legends spun, a timeless spell.
Their fabric cradles tales of old,
With magic draped in threads of gold.

Forgotten heroes, chants, and lore,
Through woven paths, their spirits soar.
Beneath the surface, tales entwined,
In every stitch, the past designed.

The echoes of their journeys sing,
As memories in the fabric cling.
In shadows cast by stories grand,
We reach to grasp the lore at hand.

So let us travel through the seams,
Where every thread ignites our dreams.
With every stitch, a world awakes,
In forgotten legends, magic breaks.

Thus weave we now, our own delight,
In fabric rich with day and night.
For history's charm shall never fade,
In every tale that we have made.

A Stitch in Time's Enchantment

In moments lost, a magic stirs,
A stitch in time, the vision blurs.
With every thread, a pathway sewn,
To worlds unknown, the heart has grown.

The needles dance with fuzzy light,
Creating sparks that chase the night.
Each stitch a spark from ages past,
A tapestry of shadows cast.

In tangled yarns, we find our fate,
With patterns drawn by hands of late.
The stitches hum a gentle song,
Where all our memories belong.

In quiet corners, fate entwines,
Through time's embrace, the soul aligns.
A stitch within the fabric's weave,
In enchantment's tale, we dare believe.

So weave we now, with threads divine,
In moments bright, let our hearts twine.
For magic calls, in every seam,
A stitch in time, a woven dream.

Echoes of Midnight Weavings

In shadows deep, where whispers weave,
A tapestry of dreams we believe.
Threads of hope in twilight's glow,
Awake the tales that only few know.

Stars dance softly in the silent night,
Guiding hearts to the realms of light.
Each thread a story, a secret told,
In the fabric of magic, bright and bold.

With every stitch, a promise bound,
In this quiet space, where dreams abound.
The loom of fate spins tales unseen,
In the midnight's hush, we chase the dream.

Fingers trace the patterns' flow,
In the realm where only dreamers go.
Each echo resonates with pure delight,
As time stands still in the spell of night.

Gleams of Craft and Enchantment

Amidst the glimmer of candle's glow,
We craft our dreams, soft and slow.
With laughter stitched in every seam,
We sew the fabric of our dream.

Enchantments spill from nimble hands,
Creating wonders on shifting sands.
Each creation holds a spark of grace,
A piece of magic in this sacred space.

Threads of silver, hues of gold,
We weave the tales that must be told.
With needle's point and careful art,
We stitch the wonders of the heart.

In shadows cast by twilight's kiss,
We find our craft, a simple bliss.
In every knot, our hopes entwined,
A testament to what we find.

Darkened Stitchings of the Heart

Within the folds of midnight's shroud,
Lies the sorrow veiled, unbowed.
Each stitch a memory steeped in pain,
In the darkened cloth, emotions rain.

With trembling hands, we sew the grief,
Searching for solace, a small relief.
Threads of heartache, woven tight,
Crafting shadows in the fading light.

In every seam, a secret lies,
A story whispered to the skies.
As we stitch the wounds of time gone by,
The heart finds strength to once again fly.

From darkness springs a flickering flame,
In the pain, we forge our name.
Through every stitch, we learn to cope,
Darkened weavings cradle hope.

Mysteries Encased in Cotton Dreams

Beneath the layers of cotton sheets,
Lies a world where starlight meets.
A maze of dreams in slumber's thread,
Woven whispers of the night ahead.

Each fold a promise, wrapped with care,
In shadows deep, mysteries flare.
As gentle breezes caress the night,
Our hopes take flight in soft moonlight.

Stitch by stitch, we unravel fate,
With every turn, we contemplate.
The stories told in woven seams,
Encased forever in cotton dreams.

In the quietude of sleep's embrace,
We find the magic of time and space.
A tapestry of wonder waits,
In the dreams we weave, our future creates.

Seamstress of Sorcery

In shadows deep, where whispers thread,
She crafts her spells with needle's tread.
Each stitch a secret, each knot a charm,
Her magic weaves, alluring and warm.

With silken strands of twilight hue,
She stitches dreams from skies so blue.
A fabric spun from hopes and fears,
Awakening wonder, drying tears.

The loom she runs, in circles wide,
Conjuring wonders, with fate as guide.
Each pattern tells of battles fought,
Of love and loss, of lessons taught.

Through ancient patterns, the flow of time,
Her artistry dances, a timeless rhyme.
In secret nooks, where shadows creep,
She stitches spells while the world sleeps.

So seek her out in twilight's glow,
Where fabrics blossom, and stories flow.
In her hands, the threads align,
The seamstress of sorcery, truly divine.

The Woven Spell of Twilight

In the twilight's embrace, where shadows dwell,
A tapestry weaves its enchanting spell.
Golden threads against the night,
Painting stories in sparkling light.

Each fiber forged from dreams and air,
Weaving wishes with utmost care.
Beneath the stars, where silence sings,
Magic dances on silken wings.

As twilight deepens, the colors blend,
A masterpiece where stories mend.
In every loop, a tale is spun,
Of ancient powers, a race yet run.

So gather 'round, in fading light,
Let the woven tales take flight.
In this enchanted, dusky realm,
The spell of twilight at the helm.

For those who seek the unseen seam,
Will find their hearts in woven dream.
A tapestry both fierce and fair,
In twilight's glow, magic fills the air.

Threads of Gloom and Glamour

In shadows cast where sorrows dwell,
Threads of gloom weave tales to tell.
With a glimmer bright, they twist and spin,
Beauty laces the darker skin.

Glistening strands of shimmering night,
Entwine with whispers of lost delight.
Yet within this delicate plight,
Lies a magic that feels just right.

With nimble fingers, the seamstress sways,
Creating fashions for darker days.
In layers veiled, with secrets bound,
Glamour blooms where shadows surround.

Through each knot, a history penned,
Gloom and glamour, together blend.
In the cool of dusk, a union rare,
Fashioned with love, beyond compare.

So wear the threads with hearts so bold,
For each stitch speaks of stories told.
In the dance of light and shadow's spell,
A journey begins where mysteries dwell.

Mystical Patterns in the Dark

Beneath the moon's enchanting gaze,
Mystical patterns begin to blaze.
In silken darkness, secrets hide,
Awaiting the heart that dares the tide.

With every stitch, the night unfolds,
A tapestry rich with dreams untold.
Whispers woven in fabric tight,
Glimmer softly, igniting the night.

In the dance of shadows, elegance sways,
Compelling echoes of ancient ways.
Each curve and line, a fate entwined,
In the realm of shadows, magic confined.

The seamstress hums a haunting tune,
With hands that craft beneath the moon.
In magic's hold, the patterns spark,
Illuminating paths through the dark.

So seek the beauty in hidden seams,
For within the night, you'll find your dreams.
A journey starts with threads unspun,
Mystical patterns, now begun.

Tapestries of the Coven's Heart

In shadows deep where secrets lay,
The sisters weave at break of day.
With whispered spells and laughter bright,
They stitch their dreams in the moonlight.

Each thread a tale, each knot a tie,
Binding hearts as the echoes fly.
Through ancient woods where magic swirls,
The coven spins their silver curls.

With eyes aglow like stars at night,
They share their fears and hearts' delight.
As woven words in harmony grow,
Together they sing what they know.

Enchantments dance in the twilight air,
All burdens shared, no weight to bear.
In tapestry rich, love's colors blend,
A sisterhood that will never end.

The Needle's Dance in Twilight's Grasp

A needle glimmers in twilight's hue,
Through fabric soft, it spins anew.
It dances lightly, stitching dreams,
In the stillness, magic gleams.

With every poke, a story unfolds,
Of whispered wishes and secrets told.
The fabric weaves both joy and pain,
In every stitch, a thread of rain.

As shadows wrap 'round the ancient trees,
The needle darts as quick as the breeze.
It finds its way through heart and soul,
Creating patterns that make one whole.

In twilight's grasp where wonders sway,
Each stitch becomes a spell to play.
With laughter ringing in the night,
The needle spins till morning light.

As dawn approaches, their work now shines,
A tapestry of dreams entwined.
In every thread, in every seam,
The echoes of the coven's dream.

Stitches of the Lunar Embrace

Under the gaze of the watchful moon,
The coven gathers, hearts attune.
Each stitch a promise, a bond renewed,
A circle of love in threads imbued.

With silken strands in silver light,
They weave their hopes into the night.
In rhythmic movements, fingers glide,
Binding together, side by side.

Whispers of magic fill the air,
Tales of the brave and those who dare.
For every shadow that darkness makes,
A stitch of light in harmony breaks.

The moonbeam's touch guides their hands,
As ancient wisdom softly stands.
In every loop, in every turn,
The fires of friendship brightly burn.

With dawn's embrace, their work complete,
A masterpiece at their feet.
In stitches bound with love so true,
The lunar light forever grew.

Secrets Woven on the Witch's Loom

In the corner of a moonlit room,
A loom awaits with tales of gloom.
With threads of twilight, soft and fine,
The witch begins her work divine.

Each secret whispered, each truth revealed,
In the fabric's fold, emotions sealed.
A tapestry rich with stories spun,
Of battles lost and victories won.

With fingers nimble, she draws each thread,
Mending the hearts that sorrowed bled.
A world of magic in every loop,
As ancient spirits begin to swoop.

From shadows dark where mysteries creep,
The loom brings forth what dreams might keep.
In colors bright, with shadows entwined,
The witch weaves wonders, both fierce and kind.

As dawn breaks soft, the work is done,
Secrets woven, stories spun.
In every fold, the past will gleam,
On the witch's loom, they share a dream.

Whispers of Darkened Threads

In shadows cast by twilight's grace,
Whispers weave a hidden place.
Secrets tangled in the night,
Silent fears take flight with fright.

Fingers dance through darkened seams,
Crafting fate with tattered dreams.
Each thread tells a tale untold,
Of hearts entwined in echoes bold.

A shiver runs through ancient trees,
Breath of magic on the breeze.
Gathering dusk in quiet breaths,
Embracing life's enchanting depths.

In the stillness, shadows sigh,
Voices linger, spirits fly.
Paths unveil where none can tread,
Beneath the weight of words unsaid.

With every knot, a promise made,
Every loop a choice displayed.
In the dark, both brave and meek,
Whispers live where shadows speak.

Spells Woven with Silver Shadows

In the hush of the silver night,
Spells unfurl in dimming light.
Around the hearth, warm and bright,
Tales of magic take their flight.

Stitches fine as spider's thread,
Crafting journeys yet to tread.
Each incantation, soft and low,
Filling hearts with sparks that glow.

Glimmers dance on fabric dreams,
Spilling forth from moonlit streams.
With every weave, time bends and sways,
Awakening forgotten ways.

In silver shadows, truths arise,
Beneath the gaze of ancient skies.
Whispers linger, secrets blend,
As magic and enchantment mend.

Woven deep in twilight's glare,
Spells arise, light as air.
Casting wonder, lighting skies,
In the night, where magic lies.

Enchanted Stitches in the Moonlight

Underneath the moon's soft glow,
Enchanted stitches start to flow.
Threads of silver, white, and gold,
Binding stories brave and bold.

With needle sharp as whispered dreams,
Sewing magic in silver beams.
Forming patterns, unseen, rare,
In each knot, a wish laid bare.

Through the fabric of the night,
Shimmers dance, a wondrous sight.
Stitched with care by hands unseen,
In the dark, a world serene.

Every twist, a tale unfolds,
Of love, and loss, and secrets told.
With every seam, the past returns,
Igniting dreams and ancient yearns.

Enchantment flows in every thread,
Whispering softly of paths ahead.
In moonlit hours, where shadows creep,
Awakened tales in silence steep.

The Sorceress's Tapestry

In a chamber where the shadows dwell,
A sorceress weaves her magic well.
Threads of fate in colors bright,
Creating worlds with pure delight.

Each stitch a secret, softly spun,
Crafting stories one by one.
Echoes of laughter, whispers of pain,
Entwined in fabric, joy and disdain.

Her fingers dance like windblown leaves,
In a tapestry that never deceives.
Imagined realms take flight and soar,
In vibrant hues, forever more.

Within each fold, an echo stays,
Of ancient powers and mystic ways.
Unraveling dreams, woven with care,
The sorceress knows her heart lays bare.

So come, behold her wondrous art,
The tapestry that speaks to the heart.
In every thread, a spark ignites,
Illuminating the starry nights.

Witches' Craft Beneath the Gleaming Sails

Upon the waves, the cauldrons boil,
Where magic stirs in cosmic toil.
Beneath the sails, the whispers blend,
As ancient secrets shift and bend.

With starlit maps and potion's grace,
The witches gather, a night's embrace.
They conjure winds with careful art,
Awakening the ocean's heart.

In every spell, the moonlight glows,
As waves caress the shore it knows.
A dance of shadows, whispers free,
In tides of dreams beneath the sea.

With feathers light and silver threads,
The laughter of the night sky spreads.
Each tranquil wave a tale retold,
Of brave hearts and treasures bold.

Their sails unfurled, they race the dawn,
A flicker of fate, a life reborn.
In magic's grip, they are entwined,
With every heartbeat, souls aligned.

Shadows of the Loom Flicker

In twilight's hush, the shadows weave,
Their fingers dancing, none perceive.
With threads of gold and midnight's shade,
A tapestry of dreams is laid.

A loom that hums with whispered tales,
Of distant lands and stormy gales.
Each knot a secret, each fold a sigh,
As time unravels, still we try.

With shadows cast upon the ground,
The weavers spin, their spirits bound.
In every dusk, new patterns form,
With love and laughter, they keep warm.

The flicker of a candle's light,
Reveals the truths that hide from sight.
In every stitch, a world awakes,
Of dreams and hopes, the loom remakes.

Though threads may fray and colors fade,
The weavers smile, unafraid.
For in each shadow's gentle sway,
A spark of magic leads the way.

Celestial Threads in the Breeze

The stars above like diamonds shine,
In cosmic dances, fate aligns.
With threads so fine, they weave the night,
As dreams take flight in silver light.

Caught in the winds, the whispers soar,
A symphony of tales, folklore.
The universe hums a soothing tune,
With every breeze, the heart's commune.

Beneath the sky, the shadows play,
In every breath, a bright ballet.
Celestial hands, so deftly skilled,
Craft moments sweet, and spirits thrilled.

In secret glades, where starlight glows,
The magic stirs, and love bestows.
Each sacred thread a promise held,
A journey told, a dream compelled.

And as the night begins to fade,
The memories dance in light and shade.
In twilight's fold, our hearts agree,
We are the threads of destiny.

Knotted Dreams of the Moonlit Sea

The moonlight spills on ocean's plane,
A silver thread in soft refrain.
With gentle waves, the whispers call,
To tangled dreams, where shadows fall.

In depths unknown, the secrets rest,
Of hearts entwined and souls expressed.
With every swell, the voices weave,
In strands of hope, we dare believe.

The sailor's heart, a restless beast,
Yearns for the tides and the night feast.
In every knot, a promise sealed,
Of all the dreams that life revealed.

Upon the waves, the echoes chase,
Reflections of a lost embrace.
Each sigh a wave, each star a tear,
In moonlit dreams, we find no fear.

So let the sea and night conspire,
To draw our hearts, to lift them higher.
For in the depths, our spirits free,
Are knotted dreams of eternity.

Whispers of Gossamer Threads

In twilight's hush, the whispers play,
A dance of light where shadows sway.
Each thread a tale of love and woe,
In gentle folds, the secrets flow.

Beneath the stars, the stories weave,
In silken strands, we dare believe.
A tapestry of dreams unfurled,
Embracing all this wondrous world.

With every stitch, a heart takes flight,
Creating colors bright as night.
In gossamer, our hopes entwine,
As moonbeams brush the fabric fine.

Through time's embrace, the echoes call,
A journey sought, we risk our all.
The weaver's hand, with magic, treads,
In silent prayers, where love embeds.

So listen close, the whispers sway,
In wind's soft breath, they find their way.
For every thread, a life concedes,
In unity, our spirit leads.

Stitches of Midnight Magic

When midnight strikes, the stars alight,
With stitches woven, pure delight.
The shadows dance, a vibrant tune,
In quiet corners, 'neath the moon.

A needle gleams in silver beams,
Crafting wonders from our dreams.
Each loop a touch of ancient lore,
Awakening magic evermore.

The fabric whispers tales untold,
Of hopes and fears in threads of gold.
In every seam, our spirits rise,
Unraveling truths in night's disguise.

So gather 'round this mystic night,
As stitches glow with whispered light.
For in this moment, hearts align,
In midnight's weave, our fates combine.

Embrace the magic, feel it soar,
In stitches wrought forevermore.
In every seam, let dreams ignite,
As we embark on journeys bright.

Enchanted Tapestry of Dreams

Within the loom of endless skies,
The threads of fate begin to rise.
An enchanted dance of colors bright,
Unfolding softly in the night.

Each dream a stitch, a story spun,
A tapestry where hearts are won.
Embroidered hopes in silken grace,
A journey shared, a warm embrace.

In vibrant hues, the visions gleam,
As night entwines with every dream.
Through whispered tales, the magic grows,
In every knot, our spirit flows.

The fabric hums with life anew,
In patterns shaped by me and you.
Together, we'll create the art,
An everlasting bond of heart.

So hold this thread, embrace the scheme,
As we embark upon a dream.
In woven realms, forever stay,
In enchanted threads, we'll find our way.

Shadows in the Moonlit Fabric

In moonlit shadows, secrets weave,
A fabric rich, it dares believe.
With silken strands of night enfolded,
The dreams of dawn, forever molded.

Eerie whispers in quiet light,
A shiver dances through the night.
Each shadow cast, a story told,
In threads of silver, brave and bold.

As crickets sing their lullabies,
The fabric shifting, never lies.
In twilight's grasp, the magic swells,
In whispered spells, the darkness dwells.

So take a thread, entwine your heart,
In shadow's realm, we'll never part.
Together here, in mystic hue,
The moonlit fabric holds us true.

Each heartbeat stitched in cosmic dreams,
In shadows deep, where silence screams.
Embrace the night, let courage rise,
In moonlit fabric, love defies.

The Weaving of Otherworldly Wishes

In twilight's embrace, where shadows dance,
A tapestry spun with a glance,
Each thread a whisper of dreams untold,
In colors of silver and strands of gold.

The moon casts a spell on the fabric of night,
Stitching wishes that take flight,
With fingers of starlight, we weave the lore,
Of realms that await just beyond the door.

A loom of enchantment, a heart's delight,
Where courage is woven with threads of light,
In the fabric of fate, we find our way,
With every stitch, we mold our day.

Glimmers of magic in every seam,
A patchwork of hopes, a dreamers' dream,
Through fibers of fate, we craft and mend,
In the weaver's world, where wonders blend.

So gather your wishes, let the needle glide,
In the realm of the unseen, let our dreams reside,
For in the weaving, we find our truth,
In the threads of light, lies eternal youth.

The Needle's Tale of Alchemy

In hands that tremble, the needle thread,
With every poke, a story spread,
Through fabric of time, we stitch and weave,
A tale of alchemy we dare to believe.

Transforming dreams from rags to rich,
With each careful stitch, we summon the witch,
Whispers of magic, in colors so deep,
In the heart of our craft, secrets we keep.

From common cloth to royal garb,
Each line, a spell, each curve, a barb,
A history woven with wisdom and care,
The needle dances, light as air.

Through trials of fabric, our souls entwined,
In patterns complex, the fates aligned,
With visions of grandeur, our spirits soar,
In the needle's tale, we seek for more.

So mark the path with threads of gold,
In the alchemist's hands, let the magic unfold,
For every creation is born anew,
In the dance of the needle, the old and the true.

Dark Lace and Enchanted Threads

In the shadows lurk, where lace takes form,
Threads enchanted weave the storm,
Whispers of secrets in fibers so dark,
Crafted intentions with a flicker and spark.

Beneath moonlit skies, the fabric sings,
A symphony spun of ethereal things,
With each delicate knot, a story to tell,
In the lace's embrace, where spirits dwell.

The touch of the needle, a beckoning call,
To weave through the night, we'll rise or fall,
In the folds of our fears, find courage anew,
For every dark lace is layered with truth.

Patterns emerge with a flick of the wrist,
Stories ensnared in a silken mist,
From shadows to light, we stitch and unfold,
In dark lace, the mysteries of old.

So gather your shadows, let magic arise,
For in enchanted threads, the heart never lies,
Through delicate stitches, embrace the dread,
In the dance of the needle, our fate is shed.

Fables Stitched in Starlight

Under the canopy of shimmering skies,
We stitch our fables with wonderous sighs,
In threads of starlight, our tales take flight,
With every heartbeat, they pierce the night.

Through cosmos vast, our dreams extend,
In the fabric of night, where fantasy bends,
Stitched with wisdom, both old and new,
In the loom of existence, our hopes accrue.

Each stitch a heartbeat, each knot a wish,
We weave our stories, our spirits they fish,
From galaxies far to shores so near,
In starlight's embrace, we conquer fear.

So dance through the patterns, let magic ignite,
In fables of wonder, we bask in delight,
For stitched in the starlight, our stories are spun,
In the tapestry woven, we shine as one.

So gather 'round, let our voices be heard,
In fables stitched softly, both spoken and stirred,
For in the threads of history, love shall reside,
In the heart of creation, let dreams be our guide.

Conjured Patterns on the Ocean's Edge

Upon the shore where secrets lie,
The waves weave tales of days gone by.
With shells as verses, and sand as ink,
I trace the patterns, and pause to think.

In twilight's glow, the horizon bends,
As dreams of merfolk dance, transcends.
With whispers soft, like ocean's breath,
They conjure life beyond sweet death.

The moon spills silver on water's skin,
Reflecting glimmers of what has been.
Each ripple carries a story's thread,
Of hopes and fears that lovers dread.

Beneath the waves' eternal sway,
Magic lingers, night turns to day.
A siren's song on the salty breeze,
Draws wanderers close, with gentle ease.

And so I wander, where dreams collide,
In the dance of the tides, I confide.
A tapestry spun from sea and sand,
I find my heart in this enchanted land.

Tidal Sorcery in Fabric's Dance

From loom to shore, the weaver's art,
Stitches intertwined, each thread a part.
The fabric ripples, a vibrant tide,
With colors that shift, where magic hides.

Tidal sorcery in delicate weave,
Patterns unfolding, a tale to believe.
Like waves that crash, each fold replies,
Whispering dreams with shimmering sighs.

Silken strands of a twilight theme,
Woven together, a painter's dream.
As night descends, their secrets gleam,
In shadows cast, the heart will scheme.

Each garment spun from a shimmered spell,
Carries the stories the ocean will tell.
With every twirl, a siren's call,
In frocks of mystique, we are enthralled.

So let the fabrics sway and spin,
As moonlit whispers draw us in.
In the dance of tides, where dreams are found,
We weave our fate on enchanted ground.

Harbors of Enchantment and Thread

In harbors safe, where whispers blend,
Stitching together both foe and friend.
A tapestry rich with laughter and pain,
Fills the sails of ships across the main.

Each thread a tale, of journeys vast,
Of fleeting moments and shadows cast.
With needles sharp and hearts that yearn,
The fires of memory flicker and burn.

Enchantments woven from sea to sky,
In colors bright that never say die.
With every knot, a promise is made,
In the fabric of time, love won't fade.

And in this harbor, dreams take flight,
As stars awaken in the deep night.
Surrounded by threads of wonder and lore,
The spirit of magic forever will soar.

So gather round, let stories unfurl,
In this realm where dreamers twirl.
For harbors stand, both legends and thread,
Cradling hopes that never go dead.

The Seamstress of Celestial Dreams

In starlit nights, a seamstress toils,
Crafting dreams where imagination coils.
With fingers deft, she shapes the skies,
Stitching magic with sparkling sighs.

Her needle threads the light of dawn,
Weaving hope where shadows are drawn.
In patterns bold, the cosmos gleams,
A realm alive with whispered dreams.

Through fabric thin, the galaxies speak,
Of love and loss, of strong and weak.
Every seam binds the heart's delight,
In the tapestry of endless night.

She dances with stars, in cosmic embrace,
Creating worlds beyond time and space.
With every stitch, a new tale spun,
In the fabric of life, she's never done.

So here's to the seamstress, quiet and wise,
Conjuring beauty beneath silver skies.
In celestial threads, we find our place,
Lost in her art, we dance with grace.

Bound by Enchantment's Threads

In shadows deep where whispers dwell,
The threads of fate weave tales to tell.
With every knot, a story grows,
Of love and loss that fate bestows.

An ancient loom, its magic deft,
Entwines our hearts, where hopes are left.
A tapestry of dreams unfolds,
In every hue, a secret holds.

The stars above in silence gleam,
As we embark upon this dream.
With stitches fine, we mend the night,
To craft a world of pure delight.

Together bound, we brave the storm,
In love's embrace, we find our form.
Each twisted thread a promise made,
In enchantment's web, we won't disfade.

So let us dance in twilight's sway,
And weave anew what keeps at bay.
For in the loom, our hearts entwine,
Forever marked as yours and mine.

Twilight's Cloak and Hidden Knots

Beneath the cloak of twilight's hue,
The secrets hide, both old and new.
In whispers soft, the night conceals,
The magic spun in quiet reels.

With silver threads and golden chain,
Our dreams reside, our hearts remain.
The knots we tie, a bond so strong,
In shadows where we both belong.

Each gentle pull, a tug of fate,
As twilight wraps us in its weight.
With every stitch, a tale unfolds,
Of courage found and love untold.

The stars take flight, their glow so bright,
As we journey through the endless night.
In knots of fate, we dance and weave,
In twilight's grasp, our souls believe.

So let us walk where shadows soar,
In twilight's cloak, we'll seek for more.
For hidden knots shall guide our way,
Through night's embrace to break of day.

The Sorcery Beneath the Stitching

In every stitch, a spark ignites,
A glimpse of magic, hidden sights.
With nimble fingers, we create,
A world of wonder, love, and fate.

The needle dances, swift and true,
In fabric's heart, our dreams imbue.
With threads of gold and silver seamed,
The sorcery of hopes redeemed.

Beneath the stitching, whispers flow,
In every seam, the magic grows.
We sew together joy and strife,
Creating patterns of our life.

The universe in fabric lies,
Each woven tale beneath the skies.
With every knot, a wish confessed,
In sorcery, our souls find rest.

So let us weave with heart and hand,
A tapestry of dreams so grand.
For in each stitch, the past shall gleam,
In sorcery beneath the seam.

Secrets Woven in Candlelight

In candlelight, the shadows play,
As secrets weave their soft array.
Each flicker speaks of tales untold,
In whispers hushed, our hearts unfold.

The waxen glow, it flickers bright,
Illuminates the threads of night.
With every flame, a vision spins,
Of hidden truths and quiet sins.

The tapestry of dreams we share,
In candle's warmth, we lay them bare.
With every weave, a bond we gain,
In secrets held, we dance through pain.

So let the light guide us anew,
In shadows deep, where love breaks through.
With every thread, a promise spun,
Secrets woven, forever one.

In twilight's glow, we find our way,
With candles bright to light our stay.
In woven lights, our souls unite,
In secret whispers of the night.

Ensnared by Fabric and Lore

In the tapestry woven of secrets and dreams,
Threads of the past whisper soft through the seams.
Curious patterns emerge in the light,
Binding the heart to the depths of the night.

Glimmers of magic ensnare the brave few,
With each whispered promise, the fabric feels new.
Stitching together the tales of our kin,
Unlocking the door to the world deep within.

Through shadows and echoes, the old stories hum,
Luring the lost to the place they belong.
Each knot tells a story, each fold holds a spell,
A realm filled with wonder where dreams weave so well.

Ghosts of the ancients dance beneath the loom,
Their laughter a melody, brushing away gloom.
In this woven embrace, we find our own path,
A journey of solace hidden midst the wrath.

Bound by enchantments, we rise with the dawn,
With courage and wisdom, our spirits are drawn.
Crafting our futures from threads of the past,
In the fabric of lore, our destinies cast.

Kites of Magic in the Darkness

In the cool evening air, the kites start to soar,
Spiraling high with enchantments galore.
Colorful tails shimmering in the night,
Dancing on whispers, a beautiful flight.

Through the silence of shadows, they weave and they twirl,
Each tug on the string a mysterious swirl.
Magic embedded in every bright hue,
Tales of the cosmos and wishes come true.

Boundless and free, they travel afar,
Wandering mystics with dreams like a star.
Floating on breezes where moonlight is cast,
Their journeys continue, both present and past.

When the darkness unfolds, and the stillness prevails,
These kites of enchantment tell wonderful tales.
Inviting the dreamers to cast out their prayers,
As the night softly cradles their hopes and their cares.

So let your own spirit take flight in the dark,
Like a kite woven brightly, ignite your own spark.
For in the embrace of the stars up above,
We find all the magic, all hope, and all love.

Woven Whispers from Beyond

In the hush of the night where shadows convene,
Woven whispers echo, mysterious and keen.
Softly they beckon from realms yet unseen,
Threads of the cosmos, in silence they glean.

From glimmers of starlight to deep ocean's sigh,
Every note carries the secrets that lie.
Mysteries thrumming, a delicate song,
Binding the heart where the lost ones belong.

Through the tapestry flowing, the stories unfold,
Of dreams that were shattered and echoes of old.
Each whisper a promise, a tale yet to weave,
Inviting the seeker to know and believe.

In shadows we gather, our spirits entwined,
The fabric of night, a solace designed.
Emerging from stillness, a chorus of grace,
Woven whispers beckon, finding our place.

So linger a while in the warmth of the glow,
Let the magic of whispers guide all that you know.
In the dance of the threads and the comfort they bring,
We're woven together, a timeless song to sing.

Starlit Seams of the Night Voyage

Under a sky woven with starlit seams,
The night sails forward, where fantasy gleams.
With each gentle wave, a promise unfurls,
Guiding the dreamers through magical worlds.

The winds whisper tales of the oceans they've seen,
Of heroes and legends, the places they've been.
A voyage of wonder, an odyssey bright,
Navigating currents bathed soft in moonlight.

Through storms and through silences, hearts brave and
true,
With sails marked by stardust, they venture anew.
Where secrets are carried on the backs of the night,
Every shimmer and sparkle ignites with delight.

For in the embrace of the vast galaxy's arms,
Lies magic and mystery, beauty that charms.
A call to the wanderers, the seekers of lore,
To traverse the horizon, forever explore.

So hoist up your sails and follow your dreams,
In the starlit embrace of the night's calming gleams.
For life's fullest treasures await on the sea,
In the voyage of dreams, you are truly free.

The Sorceress's Needlework

In shadows cast by twilight's grace,
A whisper weaves through time and space.
With needle gleaming, magic spins,
Crafting stories where the dream begins.

Each stitch, a charm, each knot, a spell,
Binding tales in a hidden dwell.
From fabric fine, her visions rise,
In colors bright, beneath the skies.

With threads of gold and silken hues,
She whispers secrets to the muse.
A tapestry of worlds untold,
In every fold, a dream to hold.

Through needle's eye, the stars align,
A weaver's heart, a soul divine.
The patterns dance, the shadows play,
In her enchanted, stitched ballet.

With each creation, realms unfold,
In wondrous tales, both new and old.
The sorceress smiles, her work complete,
In threads of magic, life's heartbeat.

Celestial Fabrics and Starlit Stories

Where stardust threads the endless night,
The fabric glimmers, soft and bright.
In cosmic hues, the heavens gleam,
Woven dreams from a silken seam.

Each comet's tail, a silver line,
Guiding hearts through realms divine.
In patterns spun by the moon's soft light,
Tales of wonder take their flight.

With every stitch, a wish cast free,
In tapestry of eternity.
The patterns rich with stories bold,
Of lovers lost and fortunes foretold.

Celestial fabrics whisper low,
As ancient secrets start to flow.
The unseen hands of time and fate,
Crafting futures in threads sedate.

Beneath the stars, new dreams take shape,
In woven realms, all fears escape.
In starlit stories, hearts entwine,
With every fabric, destinies align.

Thorns of Thread and Enchantment

In tangled threads, a prickly fate,
The thorns of magic rise and wait.
A sorceress spins her woven snare,
In delicate hands, the fraying care.

With every pull, a tale misunderstood,
Of joy entwined in shadowed wood.
Enchantments wrapped in thorny lace,
A beauty hidden, a secret embrace.

The needle pierces, revealing strife,
Yet from the pain, springs forth new life.
In darkness bound, the light will bloom,
From thorns arise, a sweet perfume.

With colors deep as the midnight sky,
A tapestry woven where dreams do lie.
In vibrant hues, the struggle sings,
Of hope reborn and the dance of wings.

Through thorns and threads, the stories weave,
In every heart, the will to believe.
Enchantress of fabric, keeper of night,
In thorny realms, she finds her light.

Midnight's Quilted Secrets

In the hush of night, where whispers dwell,
Midnight's quilt conceals a spell.
Each patch a mystery softly sewn,
In careful stitches, secrets grown.

Beneath the stars, the stories lie,
In warmth of dreams, they softly sigh.
A quilt of shadows, hearts exposed,
In midnight's embrace, they find repose.

With silver threads in moonlight's gleam,
Each piece reflects a hidden dream.
A cozy warmth wraps tales anew,
Where wishes linger, pure and true.

As midnight rolls, the tales unwind,
In every thread, a bond designed.
From cherished hopes to fears released,
In quilted trust, the heart finds peace.

With gentle hands, the sorceress seams,
Through loops of whispers and woven dreams.
In midnight's quilt, the world feels whole,
A tapestry of life, a stitched soul.

Midnight Knots and Sorcery

In the stillness where shadows creep,
Knots of magic, secrets steep.
Whispers dance on the edge of night,
Woven dreams take silent flight.

Under moon's gaze, threads align,
With every pull, the forces twine.
A tapestry of whispers spun,
In midnight's dark, all is begun.

Wands and fibers in gentle play,
Casting charms till break of day.
Starlit patterns, ancient lore,
Mysteries unlocked, forevermore.

With every knot, a story flows,
Echoes of what the starlight knows.
A spell of heart, a touch of grace,
In midnight's calm, we find our place.

As shadows bow to dawn's embrace,
Threads untangle, leave their trace.
In the light, the secrets gleam,
A magic woven in our dream.

Secrets Sewn in Twilight's Fabric

As twilight falls, the needles gleam,
Unraveling threads of a whispered dream.
In hushed confessions, shadows arise,
Each stitch a glimpse of hidden skies.

Cloaked figures dance in twilight's brush,
Weaving tales in the evening hush.
With silver twine, their secrets bind,
In fabric layers, the truth we find.

The loom of night, a sacred space,
Holding love, loss, and time's embrace.
A tapestry spun from heart and lore,
Secrets sewn forevermore.

Each thread a wish, a hope, a sigh,
Under the gaze of the twilight sky.
With threads of gold and azure blue,
We craft our fate, we weave what's true.

In the dimming light, our stories swell,
The fabric whispers the things we tell.
In twilight's weave, our voices soar,
Time stands still, and we want for more.

Charms and Yarn Beneath the Stars

Beneath the stars where dreams ignite,
Yarn and magic twine in flight.
Each loop and twist, a solemn vow,
Crafting shadows from the now.

With every stitch, a potion spun,
Charms emerging, the night begun.
In cozy corners, mysteries greet,
Unraveled tales from time's heartbeat.

Silken whispers in the cool night air,
Woven spells beyond compare.
Luminous threads in cosmic dance,
Enchanting all with their romance.

As constellations guide our hand,
Together we weave, a mystic band.
In every knot, untold desires,
We spin the warmth of summer fires.

The stars above, our guiding light,
Illuminating the threads of night.
With yarn and charm, our hearts entwined,
In the fabric of dreams, our souls aligned.

The Craft of the Dusky Weaver

In twilight's grasp, the weaver sits,
With hands that dance, the loom admits.
A tapestry rich in hues untold,
Of dreams and daring, brave and bold.

Her fingers deft, she threads the night,
In shadows deep, visions take flight.
Stitch by stitch, the world unfolds,
In dusky whispers, the magic molds.

Every pattern holds a tale of old,
Of heroes, love, and treasures gold.
In enchanted threads, a life rewinds,
The craft reveals what fate unwinds.

As dawn approaches, the colors rise,
With sunlit threads that touch the skies.
The dusky weaver smiles with grace,
Her heart now woven in time and space.

She whispers softly to the waking day,
Each crafted thread, a gentle sway.
In her embrace, all stories thrive,
Together we weave, a world alive.

Intricate Knots of Forgotten Lore

In the shadowed glade where whispers weave,
Stories lie in knots of forgotten lore.
Each thread a tale, too fragile to leave,
Entwined in dreams from times long before.

The wind carries secrets, soft as a sigh,
Echoes of magic, lost and reclaimed.
Beneath the vast canvas of an endless sky,
A tapestry waiting to be named.

With every flicker of candlelight's dance,
Ancient runes shimmer, calls from the past.
In a realm where shadows and starlight romance,
Legends awaken, their spells unsurpassed.

Here, hope threads through the intricate plait,
A guiding compass in lands of despair.
Each knot untangles the fears that await,
A bond with the stories we always will share.

So gather the threads, dear wanderer bold,
Weave your own magic in twilight's embrace.
For the knots of the past are treasures untold,
Reminding us all: in each heart, there's a place.

The Stitcher's Spell in the Gathering Dark

In the gathering dark, where silence drapes,
A stitcher sits by the flickering flame.
With needle and thread, she shapes and shapes,
Binding shadows to tales, hidden by name.

The fabric of night hums a soft tune,
As colors of dusk bleed into the grey.
With careful precision, beneath the light of the moon,
She stitches her dreams, as the hours decay.

A tapestry woven with threads of the heart,
Each knot a promise, each loop a prayer.
In this sacred craft, where sorrows depart,
The stitcher's spell fills the stillness with care.

With hands that create in the cloak of despair,
She calls forth the magic of hope deeply stored.
In the silence around, it is love that she lays bare,
With every stitched moment, her spirit restored.

So heed the soft rustle, the whispering wind,
For stories entwined will rise from the dark.
In the stitcher's realm, where dreams are pinned,
Awakens the light with each delicate spark.

Twilight's Silent Weaver

In twilight's embrace, where shadows dance,
A weaver of dreams spins her silken web.
With threads of starlight, she crafts a glance,
Ensnaring wishes that the heart may ebb.

Her fingers entwine the heart's quiet sighs,
With whispers of secrets, a soft lullaby.
Each fiber a memory, woven with ties,
A delicate tapestry where hopes learn to fly.

The night stretches wide, inviting her art,
As the moon drips silver on the folds of despair.
With every twist, she mends a lost heart,
In the silent weave, she conquers the wear.

Each thread a reminder of love left behind,
Each knot a journey through sorrow and glee.
In twilight's soft silence, her magic entwined,
Threads of enchantment like leaves on a tree.

So linger a moment, let dreams gently flow,
Through the hands of the weaver, in shadows they lay.
For twilight unveils what the heart longs to know,
In the weave of the night, where the brave find their way.

Hemming the Horizon of Mystery

At the edge of the dawn, where the day meets the night,
A tailor of secrets hems time with great care.
Gathering shadows, she binds them so tight,
Creating a cloak of enigma to wear.

With threads spun from stardust, she sketches the skies,
Each line a path, where the lost might now tread.
In her needle's sharp arc, the horizon belies,
The unspoken tales of the dreams that we've shed.

The fabric folds gently around whispered grace,
As dusk swallows light in a delicate chase.
Her patterns reveal what the heart can't embrace,
Each seam a reflection of the soul in its place.

With every stitch, she procures a new fate,
A journey for wanderers, a map for the brave.
In shadows she stitches what none can relate,
Hemming the edges of dreams we must save.

So follow the dawn on the path that she's paved,
For through the horizon lie mysteries deep.
Each hem is a promise that destiny's waved,
Inviting the seekers to wake from their sleep.

The Weave of Enigma's Embrace

In shadows deep, where whispers lie,
A tapestry of secrets, high.
Threads of twilight, spun with care,
Woven softly, in the air.

A dance of fate, with silken grace,
Each stitch a tale, a hidden place.
Around the loom, the mysteries swirl,
In darkened corners, dreams unfurl.

Moonlight glows on fabric fine,
Entwined with hopes, and dreams divine.
The weaver's hands, both sure and bold,
Crafting stories yet untold.

In every knot, a passion stirs,
A whisper of magic, in life's blurs.
With every loop, emotions rise,
The weave of enigma never dies.

So linger long, where shadows play,
On threads of night, let spirits sway.
For in this craft, hearts will trace,
The weaves of love, the embrace of grace.

Binding Sorrows with Starlit Threads

In the tapestry of night so dark,
We bind our sorrows, leave a mark.
Each thread a wish, a quiet plea,
Stitched with hope, for all to see.

Starlit pathways lead us through,
A guide for dreams that once we knew.
In the silence, hearts entwine,
Binding sorrows, where spirits shine.

With every stitch, a tear we mend,
Embroidered tales of love, not end.
Phoenix cries beneath the moon,
New dawns beckon, promise tune.

Threads of silver, whispers soft,
In twilight's arms, our spirits loft.
For in the shadows, we find light,
Binding sorrows, taking flight.

So weave with care, and never fear,
Each starlit thread draws loved ones near.
A tapestry of souls combined,
Together strong, forever aligned.

Night's Cloak and Fables Untold

Under the cloak of night's embrace,
Fables linger, time cannot erase.
Moonlit tales, like whispers glide,
In secret corners, hearts confide.

Stars are ink in the sky's book,
With every glance, take a look.
In shadows deep, stories grow,
Bound by dreams, the world we sew.

Fables of old, in silence shared,
Where laughter mingles with the scared.
From ancient ruins, wisdom flows,
In every heart, a longing glows.

So let the night your thoughts ensnare,
With fables woven in the air.
For every stitch, a journey bold,
In night's cloak, let dreams be told.

In whispers soft, with magic throng,
Create a tale, where we belong.
For under stars, our spirits mold,
In fables bright, our truths unfold.

The Art of Darkened Needlework

With needle poised, the shadows weave,
A craft of dark, where hearts believe.
In quiet corners of the mind,
The art of needlework, defined.

Each stitch a thread of whispered fears,
Embroidered tales through silent years.
In twilight's shroud, creations rise,
A dance of fabric, truth disguised.

From frayed edges, a story spins,
In shadows deep, where longing begins.
A tapestry of silent cries,
The art reveals what seldom lies.

With every knot, the heart will bleed,
Yet through the pain, we must take heed.
For darkened work brings forth the light,
In every shade, a glimpse of sight.

So wield your needle, sharp and keen,
Craft with intention, a hopeful sheen.
In darkened threads, let beauty flow,
The art of needlework, our souls bestow.